CONFERENCE CRUSHING

CONFERENCE CRUSHING

THE 17 UNDENIABLE RULES ON HOW TO NETWORK, BUILD
RELATIONSHIPS, AND CRUSH IT AT NETWORKING EVENTS
EVEN IF YOU DON'T KNOW ANYONE

BY TYLER WAGNER

"As a frequent conference attendee, one of the challenges I've had in the past is having a plan going in and a plan for after. Wagner nails the process exactly as it should happen. For a brief read (50+ pages), this book is packed with great advice, tools, and resources. I can't wait to listen to the audio book."

Adam Carroll

"The richest people in the world build their networks, while everyone else just looks for work. And with Conference Crushing, you'll get the best secrets to do it."

Dane Maxwell

"Utilizing this concise and useful book is the best way to prepare for any conference or networking event. The lessons are lasting and effective, can't recommend it enough!

Dana Reilley

"I've always thought the mark of a great book is one that you know you'll read multiple times. This is undeniably the case for Conference Crushing. Tyler's writing style is addicting; he weaves nuggets of knowledge from other books in with his own findings in a concise manner. I flew through this book and found myself feeling inspired. Not "go tweet a Marilyn Monroe quote" inspired, but actually inspired to approach uncomfortable networking situations with a confident attitude. Tyler packages a wealth of information into a short book that the reader can refer back to every time he or she is planning for a conference."

Adam Harms

"This book is a quick read that offers great advice for how to make connections, grow your network, and get ahead in your professional career. "Conference Crushing" presents an easy 17-step framework for what to do before, during, and after conferences in order to maximize your experience. A great book for entrepreneurs and business minded people looking to enhance their relationships and expand their opportunities."

Amanda Cartledge

"Very powerful, yet concise book that not only benefits conference goers, but also changes the perspective on networking and relationship building for individuals in all walks of life!"

Sarah Nail

ISBN: 1497425476
ISBN-13: 978-1497425477

www.ConferenceCrushing.com
For orders, please email: orders@conferencecrushing.com

CONTENT

ACKNOWLEDGEMENTS

The following people continue to inspire me everyday. Thank you for adding so much value to this world and helping me to do the same.

Jayson Gaignard, Chandler Bolt, James Roper, Sara Stibitz, Ida Fia Sveningsson, Dane Maxwell, Adam Carroll, Timothy Augustine, Mitch Matthews, UJ Ramdas, Ameer Rosic, Alex Ikonn, Michael Gebben, James Wallace, Chris Plough, Chad Mureta, Tim Ferriss, James Altucher, Dan Martell, Lewis Howes, Derek Halpern, Shaa Wasmund, Joey Coleman, and Clay Hebert.

DOWNLOAD THE AUDIOBOOK AND ACTION GUIDE FREE!

READ THIS FIRST

I've found that readers have the most success with my book when they use the Action Guide as they read.

Just to say thanks for buying my book, I'd like to give you the Audiobook and Action Guide 100% FREE!

Download the Action Guide and Audiobook for FREE at
ConferenceCrushing.com/Actionguide

FOREWORD

I'll never forget the day my biggest hero in business, Jason Fried, told me he was proud of my business.

> **Jason:** *How many customers do you have on your platform?*
> **Me:** *Around 100.*
> **Jason:** *What do you charge a month?*
> **Me:** *Around 100... $10,000 per month in revenue.*

I thought it was pathetic. I thought it was lousy. I thought I was on the wrong path. I doubted myself. My business. Wondered if I'd ever "arrive."

> **Jason:** *Dude that is awesome, you must be proud.*

It floored me. Happiness shot through my entire body. It gave me confidence I was on the right path.

> **Jason:** *You should look into doing coupons, it's exploded our business.*

I did. And today my business is vastly greater than it was when I met him. Not just because of the coupons though ... It was because of conversations I had with Jason and people like him.

These conversations took place backstage at conferences.

When everyone else was paying big money to listen to guys like this speak, I was emailing the conference coordinators asking to volunteer and be the "assistants" to these big names.

As an assistant, I walked them from the elevator to the stage. It was a rough job.

Now, these conversations happen all the time without being at conferences. Now, these are the circles I am fortunate enough to play in. The richest people in the world build their networks, while everyone else just looks for work.

And with Conference Crushing, you'll get the best secrets to do it.

Dane Maxwell
Partner at TheFoundation.com | Start A Business From Nothing

TRANSFORM YOURSELF TO TRANSFORM THE CONFERENCE

When I walked through the doors of my first conference it felt like my first plane ride as a young boy; I was nervous, but very excited. I had enough business cards to fill up the room. I was ready to grow personally, professionally, and build some amazing relationships. As the day went on, I was feeling pretty good; I met a couple new people, took some notes from the speakers, and handed out as many business cards as I could. Over the next two days I spoke to a couple more people, handed out still more cards, and took more notes. I was learning tons of implementable information and meeting a lot of new people. The feeling was great, but once the conference was over something just didn't feel right. A few weeks went by and I found myself in the same position I was in prior to the conference.

I went to that conference to build relationships, grow personally, and become more successful. Why didn't any of that happen for me? We've all been this person at a conference; we've all left an event feeling like we could have done more. On the other hand, we've all seen the person at the event who befriends everyone, and afterwards you continue to hear about the success he or she is having.

Business conferences, personal growth events, and similar gatherings are an expensive investment of our time and money. However, every event has the potential to change your life. Every event offers you an abundance of opportunities. The problem? Most people are not maximizing their ROI (return on investment) at these events. They simply don't know how to.

The reality is, none of us were ever taught how to succeed at these events. No one sits you down to explain how it works, and you certainly don't learn this in any college course.

After the disappointing outcome of my first conference, I knew something had to change. As Mark Twain said, "Whenever you find yourself on the side of the majority, it is time to pause and reflect."

If I wanted to get more out of my investment, I had to change my approach to conferences and networking events. I started reading tons of books, articles, and blogs on the subject. After gathering all of the information I could get my hands on, I realized successful networking came down to one thing: providing value for other people.

When I walked into my first conference, I wasn't thinking about how to be of service to others. Like most of us, I was thinking about meeting people who could help me. I was wrong.

That simple mind-set changed the way I interacted with people not just at conferences, but in my every-day life. I started testing that knowledge and finding out what worked and what didn't. Through my failures and successes I perfected the process, and now I'm sharing everything I've learned with you. All of the best information is compiled into this book with a guide on how to take action.

We all know attending networking events can be a key component to our success. Imagine making an investment and knowing what your return would be beforehand.

You might be thinking… "That sounds a little like insider trading." You would be right. Luckily, this kind is not illegal. This is the book that shows you how to maximize every event you attend so your personal growth accelerates.

We'll cover the following:

- **Conference How-To:** prepare yourself with the 17 rules on what to do before, during, and after attending a conference.

- **Conference Hacks:** learn how to get into a conference for free and get the most value out of every event.

- **Networking Tools and Tips:** learn how to build long-lasting relationships and grow your network.

Just as John C. Maxwell said, "Your network is your net worth." Conference Crushing makes it easy for you to maximize your network with clear and actionable advice.

Because you'll know exactly what to do before, during, and after every conference, you'll leave every event feeling fulfilled and energized with new and exciting direction on your path to success.

Using the tactics I've outlined in this book, I've met thought leaders like Tim Ferriss, Marc Ecko, James Altucher, and many more. I've received free or discounted attendance to some of the best networking events around the country and internationally, built long-lasting relationships with some of the most amazing entrepreneurs in the world, and gained considerable amounts of knowledge and opportunities. From running a successful $65,000+ business at the age of 20 to helping oversee $1,000,000 in business by 21, all of my success roots from my process for getting the most out of conferences and networking events.

Don't continue to be the person who does the same thing as everyone else and only makes a few friends at these gatherings. Be the person everyone talks about at the conference. Be the person everyone wants to see succeed. Be part of the minority of movers and shakers who take immediate action and leave a lasting impact. The longer you wait to implement these strategies, the more opportunities you'll miss. If you read through the material and implement the strategies I've laid out, I promise you'll become a part of that minority.

If you are already 100% satisfied with your knowledge, career, network and everything else in your life, then maybe you don't need this book. For the rest of us, we can always be improving. All you have to do is commit to learning and implementing a different way of doing things. It starts here.

SECTION 1

BEFORE THE CONFERENCE

DEFINE WHO YOU ARE

"YOU'VE GOT TO FIND YOURSELF FIRST. EVERYTHING ELSE'LL FOLLOW." - CHARLES DE LINT

 We recently spoke about the importance of providing value to others. Understanding and defining who you are is a crucial part of providing value. In this case, defining who you are means knowing which skills, talents, and knowledge you bring to the table. Having a firm grasp on who you are in this sense will make it easier to see opportunities for providing value to others.

By taking the time to do this, the knowledge will be readily accessible for you at the conference. Use the worksheet below as an aid to come up with what you love to do, successes you've had, skills you have, and how you can add value to others. All of these can be anything. Don't sabotage yourself into thinking you aren't valuable or don't have many skills to share with others. Chances are, you're wrong. This is your time to brag about yourself. Have fun with it.

ME:

WHAT I LOVE TO DO	MY SUCCESSES	MY SKILLS	HOW I CAN ADD VALUE TO OTHERS
Help others achieve success	Mentoring students to run successful businesses	Leadership, communication, managing others, and marketing	Provide them with information and real life examples on how to be successful in these categories, look for opportunities to help them personally
Brighten people's day	Calling my mom just to say "I love you," letting friends know I am thinking of them, going out of my way to make someone I don't know smile, helping those around me become better	High energy, drive, creating happiness in others, funny (some may disagree), giving encouragement, contagious energy	Have high energy and passion when talking with them, giving constant encouragement and assistance, making others smile, giving compliments
Travel	Have been all through the U.S., Canada, Europe, and parts of Africa	Enjoying every moment of life, trying new things, taking risks, focusing on the journey and not the destination	Share funny travel experiences, give travel advice, help them take the leap to go on a new and exciting adventure personally

YOU:

WHAT I LOVE TO DO	MY SUCCESSES	MY SKILLS	HOW I CAN ADD VALUE TO OTHERS

INVESTIGATE

"RESEARCH IS CREATING NEW KNOWLEDGE."
- NEIL ARMSTRONG

 The more you know about everyone attending the conference, the better off you'll be. Start by researching the coordinator(s), then influential speakers, and then the influential attendees. In this case, influential means two types of people: those you can help, and those who can help you. This can take some time, and I'm not telling you to research every single person who will be at the event. However, if you have the time to research, the more the better.

Finding information on the coordinator(s) and speakers should be relatively easy. If the coordinator(s) don't provide you with an attendee list, shoot them a quick email or phone call. Let them know how excited you are for their event and that you'd like an attendee list so you can make the absolute most of your attendance.

Once you have everyone's name, you can start by looking them up on Google, Facebook, LinkedIn, and Twitter. As you research, you'll most likely come across more ways you both can add value to each other. I recommend keeping track of your research and highlighting anything you and the other person have in common. People post all kinds of information about themselves, so it'll be easy to find out about their passions, career, hobbies, and anything else you feel is relevant. Maybe you have someone in mind you'd like to meet at the conference. Just knowing this person likes to play golf can give you an idea of what they're like and help you understand them that much more. Any information you find is helpful because it will help you start and continue a conversation with them.

If you know the email addresses of any of the coordinator(s), speakers, or attendees, Install *Rapportive* to your computer and follow the necessary steps to link it with your email. Open up a window to compose an email and plug in the person's email address. After this, wait a few moments. Another small window will appear with a picture of the person and links to other sites the email address is associated with such as Facebook, LinkedIn, Twitter, AngelList, and more. Now you have all of the links to their information in one place.

I know you're thinking, "This sounds like you're telling me to be a stalker." Don't think of it as stalking, think of it as information-gathering with a purpose. Your goal is to provide value for them and for yourself, not to be creepy.

DEFINE YOUR WHY

"HE WHO HAS A WHY
TO LIVE FOR CAN BEAR ALMOST ANY HOW."
- FRIEDRICH NIETZSCHE

You paid money for this conference. It's essential to discover exactly what you want from it. It's time to dig deeper into your WHY to enhance your focus at the conference and achieve your goals. Before you go to your event, you need to have a concrete plan. This will give you more focus and keep you motivated.

When I went to a conference for entrepreneurs, one of my goals was to get out of my comfort zone and talk to some of the speakers. That's pretty vague. If I'd left that goal as is, it probably would have never been accomplished because there was no metric for success. Instead, I made this concrete by picking three presenters in particular. By having three people in mind, it was easy to see my progress and achieve my goal.

For a goal to be powerful it must be measurable. Think about the goal, the smaller steps necessary to accomplish it, and your desired outcome from the accomplishment. The worksheet below will help you create clear and actionable steps to achieve your goals. Keep in mind how you can add value to others throughout this process. As you're preparing, keep your goals in mind and don't forget to bring this sheet from the Action Guide with you to the event.

Here's an overview of your goal table for the conference. Continue to the next page to see an example of my goals, action steps, and desired outcomes from a previous conference. After you've seen my example, it's time for you to take action!

GOAL

ACTION STEPS

DESIRED OUTCOME

GOAL ACHIEVED (Y/N)

NEXT STEP(S)

PEOPLE I MET

HOW CAN I HELP THEM

HOW CAN THEY HELP ME

FOLLOW-UP METHOD

ME:

GOAL	ACTION STEPS	DESIRED OUTCOME
Talk to Tim Ferriss, James Altucher, and Ryan Holiday	1. Reach out to them before conference 2. Be aware of when they are speaking at event 3. When opportunity arises go for it (don't let fear defeat me)	Sincerely thank them and expand my comfort zone. Let them know how much value they have added to my life from their work.
Help five people become more comfortable and open at the conference	1. Take notice of people who are standing alone or seem nervous 2. Engage in a conversation with them 3. Brighten their day	All five people become more comfortable at the event and maximize their ROI. I created five more strong relationships and maybe they will use my services to help them with future events
Learn best practices for creating valuable and engaging content. Have a list of five things I can implement after the conference.	1. Create list of speakers / attendees that are authors, bloggers, etc. from my research 2. Reach out to them before conference 3. Be aware and attend any talks on the subject 4. Add value to the list before and during conference 5. Talk to them at event and ask them about their early struggles with writing and what they learned through their journey. 6. Take notes and put together the list of five things I can implement	Leave the conference feeling confident in my content creating abilities. Take action on the list of five things I can implement and add value to others through my content

YOU:

GOAL	ACTION STEPS	DESIRED OUTCOME

SURPRISE EVERYONE

"RELATIONSHIPS ARE THE HALLMARK OF THE MATURE PERSON." - BRIAN TRACY

The key to relationships is to build them before you need them. By reaching out to the people who will be at the conference, you'll establish connections and build rapport well before you meet them. You'll already know people at the event, which will help with any pre-conference jitters you have. And you never know what could come of a simple introductory email.

A little less than a year ago, I stumbled across a conference called *MastermindTalks* on Facebook. I went to the website and it really caught my interest. If you're an entrepreneur or aspiring entrepreneur, you'll understand when you visit the website - *mastermindtalks.com*. At the time, I was a college student and couldn't afford it, so I reached out to Jayson (the founder) via email.

I was enthusiastic about his event, telling him how awesome I thought it would be. I told him about my interests in entrepreneurship and if he needed help with anything, and I stressed anything, I would do it. It didn't even matter to me if he asked me to do something that didn't involve me attending the event, I was just excited about it.

What happened after sending just one email?

Jayson responded and accepted my offer to help. In return, I attended the event for free, I met all of the speakers and attendees, made amazing friendships, and gained an immeasurable amount of knowledge. What else? Jayson and I became great friends and I had the opportunity to intern under his leadership for three months. The experience changed my life and I'm honored to call him my friend. I'll also be attending this year's event...maybe I'll see you there!

All of that came from one email. I offered to provide value to the organizer of a great event, and he took me up on my offer. Without providing value first, I never would have had the opportunity to attend a life-changing event that was way out of my financial reach. The power of reaching out can't be overstated. You never know what could happen.

Start by looking into your own network for introductions. If you notice someone in your network knows the coordinator, a speaker, or one of the attendees, have them introduce you before reaching out. This gives you instant credibility and makes the introduction easier.

Since you've done your research, reaching out to both speakers and attendees shouldn't be too hard. Send an email to the speaker showing appreciation for their work, and explain how they've helped you (if they have). By doing this, you've instantly provided value for them. End the email telling them that you're looking forward to meeting them at the event. Don't ask them to help you or go out of their way to do anything. Depending on their response, you can choose to keep the conversation going or just wait to continue at the event. If you do decide to respond back, make sure to keep providing as much value as you can. If they don't respond, no worries. This is just a soft introduction before the event.

The previous research you did will help you reach out to your fellow attendees, as well. Send an email to all attendees with the speaker research you compiled in rule #2. When I did this for MastermindTalks, it worked so well that I became close friends with a group of attendees before the conference even began. By doing this, you've delivered value for everyone before even meeting them. People don't mind helping people who've already helped them. You should know though, word might spread fast about you; you may become just as popular as one of the speakers at the conference.

GET INTO THE CONFERENCE MINDSET

"ONCE YOUR MINDSET CHANGES, EVERYTHING ON THE OUTSIDE WILL CHANGE ALONG WITH IT."
- STEVE MARABOLI

 This is the last rule to be followed before you attend the conference. Getting into the conference mindset ties everything together. When you follow this rule, you'll notice considerable positive changes in your performance at the event.

What are you **Grateful** for?

Affirmations for Conference

Visualize yourself achieving your goals and adding value to others

Extend Invitations= Invite friends to hold you accountable for goals

You can start this process as far in advance before the conference as you'd like.

At the very least, I recommend doing it the day before and the morning of the conference. I like to start a week before the first day of the conference; by the time I get there, I'm crystal clear on everything.

Let's break the process down so you know exactly how to get in the mindset.

1. Start by thinking about, or writing down, all of the things you're grateful for in your life right now, the things you already have. Spend just two minutes on this and jot them down. Too often we focus on what we don't have. When you walk into an event focused not on what you need but on the abundance you already have, you'll feel more relaxed and happy. Not only will you be more relaxed, but other people will gravitate toward your positivity. Gratitude is the key to happiness.

2. Next, write personal affirmations for the conference. One of my favorite books, The Five Minute Journal, by Alex Ikonn and UJ Ramdas, describes an affirmation as a statement describing what you want in your life in the present tense. Some examples of affirmations could be: "I am self-confident," "I achieved all my goals at the conference," or "People love to be around me." When you write personal affirmations, your brain is primed to build this belief. After you've written them down, start saying them aloud to yourself to cement this idea in your mind. Affirmations are extremely powerful. When I attended MastermindTalks, I was lucky enough to meet Chad Mureta from App Empire. While having a great conversation, he told me he had made positive affirmations a part of his daily routine. He would tell himself, over and over again, he was an app millionaire for an hour every day before he even had a successful app on the market. It obviously worked for Chad; it can work for you. You might be thinking, "I don't have an hour every day to do this." You don't need an hour. Practice your affirmations during your morning routine by saying them aloud while you shave or do your makeup.

3. Take some time to visualize yourself achieving your goals and adding value to others at the conference. Visualize talking with an influential person you want to speak with.

Visualize yourself as relaxed and calm during this conversation, and see yourself and the person you're talking with enjoying the interaction. Visualizing success helps you to obtain it.

4. The last part of this process is what really ties it all together: tell your friends all about your goals. When you tell your friends you're going to do something, chances are you'll do it! Nobody likes to let themselves or other people down. By having accountability partners for your goals, you just can't lose. You won't want to tell your friends you got lazy and didn't take action on one of your goals, will you?

ME:

GRATEFUL	AFFIRMATIONS	VISUALIZE	EXTEND
My loving and supportive family	I am a person of value and people love to be around me		Thomas Ayling
My relationships	My network is continuously growing		Alex Ventresca
My confidence and courage	My contagious energy helped five people get out of their comfort zone and increase their ROI at the conference		Colin Wagner

YOU:

GRATEFUL | AFFIRMATIONS | VISUALIZE | EXTEND

At this point, you should feel more prepared to tackle a conference than you've ever felt in your life. Enough planning and visualizing - let's make it happen! In the next section you'll learn how to maximize your ROI while at the conference. To be able to do this effectively, the first five rules are a must. Don't skip them, because they lay the groundwork for success at your event. You'll start to see dramatic results if you put in the time.

SECTION 2

DURING THE CONFERENCE

UPGRADE
YOUR COMMUNICATION

**"THE SINGLE BIGGEST PROBLEM IN COMMUNICATION IS
THE ILLUSION THAT IT HAS TAKEN PLACE."
- GEORGE BERNARD SHAW**

 I promise not to bore you with anything along the lines of eye contact or posture, but we do need to talk about the best ways to communicate. Now, let's define the word communication. Communication is the process of transferring signals and messages between a sender and receiver through various methods. It's also the mechanism we use to establish and modify relationships. Communication is a two-way process; that means you not only need to send your message clearly, but you need to understand the messages of the person with whom you're speaking. The goal of networking and building relationships is to help people. To do so, you must understand their needs first. The research you did on the conference speakers and attendees makes this task much easier, but let's talk about how to get the most out of your interactions in a face-to-face setting.

Have you heard of the rule of 55-38-7? Albert Mehrabian, Professor Emeritus of Psychology at UCLA, studied verbal and nonverbal messages in communication. He theorized that the impact of any interaction is 55% visual, 38% sound (as in tone or speed of voice), and only 7% what you actually say.

This means the way you present yourself visually has more of an impact than the actual words you say.

Giving the impression of confidence starts with a visual impression. A great way to accomplish this is by wearing something that is unique, but also comfortable for you. Practice standing with your arms open, hands relaxed at your side, knees flexed, and feet about 8-10 inches apart. Our hard-wiring leads us to subconsciously trust symmetry; when you stand this way, you're presenting a symmetrical figure. The more you practice this, the more natural it will feel. You'll be sending a message that you're approachable, open, and trustworthy in a conference setting.

In How To Talk To Anyone, Leil Lowndes discusses what to do when you first meet someone. Treat them like an old friend. Make them feel like the only person in the room and give them your undivided attention. Something to keep in mind with first impressions: try to be as positive as possible. Use the words you, we, us, and our whenever it is appropriate. When used consistently, these words will make you both feel like you're working together and are already friends. Also, make sure to not point out someone's bloopers. If the person you're talking with says something weird, misspeaks, or anything of that nature, act as if nothing happened and keep talking like a true friend would.

Your goal is to establish and continue to build relationships, which means you need to get to know the other person on a deeper level. Without making a human connection with them, your message will not have the same level of power. The simplest way to do this? Practice asking open-ended questions to get the other person talking. For example, you wouldn't want to ask, "How do you like the conference so far?" That's a fairly closed question with an easy answer. It just doesn't invite conversation, and you learn little about them from their answer. People tend to remember a conversation as a good one if they get to talk about themselves, so let them. Remember to really listen to the other person when they are speaking. Ask follow-up questions, and maybe even take some notes. If you choose to take notes, don't feel weird about it. All you have to do is let the person know that you are really interested in what they are saying and you want to make sure you don't miss anything.

To help you listen to the best of your ability remember that the word "LISTEN" rearranged is "SILENT." To help you further build credibility with someone you've just met, let them know of other attendees they should meet. If you're able to do this during your first interaction with them, you'll demonstrate you were listening very intently.

People also love to hear nice things said about them. Take every opportunity to compliment someone you've met, whether directly or indirectly. Even if you're complimenting someone who's left the conversation, it may get back to them. At the same time, the new group you're talking to will take notice of your generosity. Everyone loves compliments; if they overhear you singing their praises, their trust in you will grow, and your relationship will be off to a great start.

DEFINE WHAT NOT TO DO

"THERE IS NOTHING QUITE SO USELESS, AS DOING WITH GREAT EFFICIENCY, SOMETHING THAT SHOULD NOT BE DONE AT ALL."
- PETER F. DRUCKER

 To keep yourself on track with your goals and maximize your attendance at the conference, it's important to know what to avoid. The list below will keep you in check. Think of this as a challenge; the more of these you avoid, the more goals you can achieve. There are obviously many more than appear on my list, so feel free to add a few if you'd like.

CONFERENCE DON'T DO'S

Don't let fear keep you from talking to other people

Don't fool yourself and think you can memorize everything without taking notes

Don't focus on quantity when networking

Don't be distracted by food or drink

Don't hand business cards to people you haven't had a conversation with yet

Don't ask yes or no questions

Don't ask only work or career-related questions

Don't forget to keep track of people you intend on following up with

Don't waste time on your phone or computer

Don't gossip about others at the event

(insert your own)

(insert your own)

(insert your own)

BE PRESENT AND AWARE

"FOREVER IS COMPOSED OF NOWS."
- EMILY DICKINSON

 The more present we are in life, the more we will get out of every experience. With everything going on around you and all of the new people you'll be meeting, it can be hard to stay focused at times. There will be times when you feel like checking out, burying your nose in your phone, or reading your favorite blog. Resist that urge. Stay in the present moment and maximize the limited amount of time you have.

Where awareness goes, energy flows. While at the conference, don't lose track of the goals you set. Review the worksheet from rule two periodically. Keeping yourself up-to-date with the goals you've achieved while in attendance makes it easier to focus and achieve the goals you haven't.

GET OUT OF YOUR COMFORT ZONE

"ONLY THOSE WHO WILL RISK GOING TOO FAR CAN POSSIBLY FIND OUT HOW FAR ONE CAN GO."
- T.S. ELIOT

 Taking greater risks leads to the possibility of greater rewards. Knowing how to take risks (and being comfortable with them) is important in every aspect of life, and it's no different with conferences and events. I guarantee some of your goals - if not all of them - can only be accomplished by you taking some sort of risk. You took some risks to get to where you are now. Keep taking them and you'll bring yourself to the next level.

Confidence is not a requirement for getting out of your comfort zone. I'm sure you've heard the phrase, "Fake it till you make it." Your behavior affects your thoughts, and pretending to be confident by taking on the mindset and body language of a confident person, will actually make you become confident. Faking it is not a bad thing. Remember, we all have moments when we need to fake confidence.

When I was at MastermindTalks it took me a while before I worked up the courage to speak to Tim Ferriss. His books had literally changed my life and I really looked up to him. I was nervous and almost talked myself out of it. But I did it anyway.

Taking that first step was hard, but it made starting conversations with others that much easier. I know it can be hard, but just start with one conversation, and you'll be on a roll.

In a conference setting, you may see someone who looks as if they don't know where they're going. Or, you might see someone standing alone with that uncomfortable oh-god-I-don't-know-who-to-talk-to look on their face. Take the first step out of your comfort zone and go greet that person to see if you can help with anything. By focusing on delivering value to others, your fear will disappear because your mind will become focused on them and not yourself. This will take you a matter of two minutes, and the other person will feel comfortable coming up to you later on at the event.

Another way to break out of your comfort zone is to take the opportunity to ask questions. If the speaker opens it up to questions or comments, be sure to speak up. If you've been listening, taking notes, and comprehending what the speaker is saying, you'll easily be able to come up with an intelligent comment or question. Asking questions not only gets you answers, but has the added benefit of drawing the attention of everyone in the room, including the speaker. Even if you're nervous, only good can come out of speaking up.

If there's a speaker you'd like to meet, but you're unsure how to approach them, start by keeping tabs on where they are. If you see a speaker exit, wait a moment, then follow them out (you can fake a phone call and wait in the lobby). Wait to "casually" run into them before they go back into the event. Remember, people like to talk about themselves. Successful people, in particular, like to talk about their early struggles. Just ask them some questions about their start-up days and the conversation will be off to a good start.

Sometimes to make miracles happen we just need to jump in. Fear is really the only thing holding us back. It's okay to acknowledge your fears, but make sure you move past them. Don't let your fears turn into regrets.

PARTICIPATE AS MUCH AS POSSIBLE

"YOU CAN'T BUILD A REPUTATION ON WHAT YOU ARE GOING TO DO." – HENRY FORD

Most conferences don't make attending everything mandatory. Why would they? You paid for this...it's up to you to show up. I've watched tons of people leave a conference early or skip parts they think won't provide value. Do not waste your time. These events are opportunities. If you're unsure about a part of the conference, then go check it out. The more you participate, the more people you'll meet. Be the first one at the conference every morning and the last one to leave every night. This way, you don't miss out on any opportunities.

Since we're talking about opportunities...isn't the event coordinator usually there before all the attendees arrive? By getting up one hour earlier, you can create one-on-one time with the coordinator of the event. Show up early and offer to help with any set up needs they might have.

Try becoming an event coordinator yourself and plan your own event. Don't wait to hear what's happening, be proactive and take control. Get people together for breakfast or dinner, or maybe drinks after the conference. Since you've spoken to many different kinds of people, you should have an idea of who would blend well in a group setting.

Keep the group small; intimate groups make it easier to get to know one another.

Keep in mind that some of the best opportunities to build strong relationships happen at night when the conference is over, so don't sack up too early or you'll miss out on some valuable time. Catch up on sleep later; you only have a few days, or maybe even hours, at your event. Make the most of them.

FALL IN LOVE WITH PEOPLE

"THE GREATEST GIFT YOU CAN GIVE TO OTHERS IS THE GIFT OF UNCONDITIONAL LOVE AND ACCEPTANCE."
- BRIAN TRACY

 People truly are fascinating. As Ralph Waldo Emerson said, "In my walks, every man I meet is my superior in some way, and in that I learn from him." We are all students and teachers of one another. When you fall in love with people, you open yourself up to what they can teach you. In turn, you give them your undivided attention, which makes them feel like they're the only person in the room. You probably know how this feels; it's a feeling of importance and appreciation.

When you fall in love with people you inevitably act as a host towards them. If you want people to have a good time meeting you, you need to have a good time meeting them. Susan RoAne, author of How to Work a Room: The Ultimate Guide to Making Connections In-Person and Online, writes that according to research on shyness, 90% of people are uncomfortable in a group setting. This means nearly everyone around you is just as nervous as you are. Now that you know this, your job becomes making others in the room feel comfortable. The more you make others feel welcome and comfortable, the more they will want to be around you.

BUILD THE FOUNDATION FOR STRONG RELATIONSHIPS

"TRY NOT TO BECOME A MAN OF SUCCESS, BUT RATHER TRY
TO BECOME A MAN OF VALUE."
- ALBERT EINSTEIN

 According to research conducted by Harvard University, The Carnegie Foundation, and The Stanford Research Institute, technical skills and knowledge account for 15% of the reason you get a job, keep a job, or advance in a job. People skills account for the other 85% of your job success.

The best way to build a strong foundation for a relationship with someone you just met is by being vulnerable, authentic, and going out of your way to add value to that person's life.

VULNERABILITY+   AUTHENTICITY+   GIVING/ADDED   FOUNDATION
                                    VALUE=   FOR STRONG
                                                    RELATIONSHIP

Vulnerability opens up trust. When you let your guard down and just open up to the other person, it opens up the conversation to new possibilities. It helps the person you're talking with open up as well.

Building trust is a key part to building a relationship. When you're vulnerable with another person, you're taking the first step by showing you trust them.

Authenticity also builds trust. Being authentic means being 100% honest about who you are. Too often we think we need to put up a front and act a certain way to fit in or be accepted, when in reality the act just creates a barrier to true connection. Drop the front and be yourself. You might not always be comfortable, but the connections you establish will be real.

Adding value to someone the first time you meet them is a great way to get their attention and ensure they'll remember you. This usually leads to two possible outcomes. First, they might feel the need to reciprocate and find out how they can be of value to you. Second, they might wonder what else you can do for them down the road considering you have delivered value so quickly. Either way, they'll be thinking about ways to continue to build the relationship.

Keep these three building blocks in mind while you work the conference. If you can consistently open yourself up, be real, and contribute to those around you, you'll have a strong foundation for your new relationships.

TAKE NOTES (PLEASE!)

"HE LISTENS WELL WHO TAKES NOTES."
- DANTE ALIGHIEIRI

 No one loves this part, but taking notes is essential, even if you find it boring or tedious. Write down information you hear from speakers, and the highlights of conversations with people you meet. There's so much going on at a big event; it's easy to lose track of the massive amounts of information you take in over the course of a day, not to mention multiple days. Jotting things down will help you remember everything.

After the conference is over, you'll be using these notes to follow-up with people in a number of ways. An easy way to continue to provide value is to send your notes to all of the attendees. You'll continue to help other people, and they'll certainly remember you. Keeping track of your conversations will prevent you from forgetting anything, and you'll be able to add a personalized touch to all of your follow-ups.

Good notes make follow-up easy, and it will be easier for you to connect people when the opportunity comes. You might go back to these notes, realize you know someone in your network who can help the person you've just met, and make an introduction. You'll find connecting one person with another in your network is beneficial for everyone involved. Conferences put those opportunities on steroids if you take advantage of them. Make a promise to yourself to take notes so you don't miss out on a chance to help yourself or someone else later on.

RULE 14

WRITE HANDWRITTEN LETTERS

"THE WRITTEN WORD ENDURES, THE SPOKEN WORD DISAPPEARS." - NEIL POSTMAN

 When's the last time you received a handwritten thank you letter? Do you remember it? I bet you do, and I bet you know exactly where it is. One handwritten letter takes five minutes, but the impact has the potential to last a lifetime.

The response I've received from giving out handwritten thank you letters has been tremendous. People receive so few handwritten letters; when they do, it feels like it's their birthday. More than likely, they'll keep it on their desk, on their refrigerator, or maybe somewhere else in plain view. The point is: they keep it. They'll see it and be reminded of you every single day. Take the time to write these letters. They can make a huge difference in your life.

Here's a letter I recieved a while back...guess where I keep it?

Thanks for the inspiration & motivation to get outside my comfort zone, grow my network & never give up on my goals.

Tyler,

Thanks for being such an unbelievable inspiration to me over the past year & a half. From student painter days (where I would do anything I could to beat you) to now, ~~to~~ you've constantly motivated & pushed me to be the best I can be. I wouldn't have ran such a big business if it wasn't for you keeping my butt in gear. Just wanted to say thanks for doing what you do. It's been a blast hanging out, learning & always being inspired by your contagious energy this past 1 1/2 years. Looking forward to many more memories! /CB

Keep this format in mind when writing your thank you notes:

- Start by thanking them. For example, thank them for their time, their input, or even thank them for the excellent conversation.

- Tell them what you learned from them or how they provided value to you. One or two sentences is sufficient, there's no need to go into lengthy detail.

- Tell them how you're going to implement what you learned, or how it will benefit you in the future.

- Offer to help them with their needs, and try to close the letter in a way that starts a discussion. Try to be specific with ways you can help them. If you aren't specific, you're actually putting the work on them to figure out how you can help them.

Keep in mind, your letters must be genuine and authentic. They have to be real. Don't just write them in hopes of benefiting yourself. If the person helped you in any way, thank them, and be sincere about it. Sincerity goes along way.

If possible, give the letter to them in person. This will be more difficult if this is only a one day event, but it's still doable. If the conference is more than one day, really push hard to make this happen. If you've been taking notes, you can refer to those when writing your letters. This doesn't just apply to speakers and organizers. Any attendee who helped you is also just as deserving of a letter.

If you do plan to give your letters in person, be careful not to mix the cards up and give out the wrong one. This sounds simple, but if you have multiple thank you letters in your pockets it can be tricky at times. While at an event, I once handed a speaker the wrong letter and then had to take out a handful of 10 other letters to find the one with his name on it. It's funny now, but it was extremely awkward at the time and I recommend avoiding that situation.

SECTION 3

AFTER THE CONFERENCE

TIME TO REFLECT

> "WHAT YOU GET BY ACHIEVING
> YOUR GOALS IS NOT AS IMPORTANT AS WHAT YOU
> BECOME BY ACHIEVING YOUR GOALS."
> - HENRY DAVID THOREAU

 What you do after the conference is just as important, if not more important, than what you did at the conference. If you're going to maximize the value of the event to its fullest potential, you need a system to organize the information you gathered. It's important to review the goals you set when preparing for the event.

Go over your goal sheet from rule number three and fill in the next two parts. Did you achieve your goals? Did you meet the people you wanted to meet? If so, congratulate yourself. You put a lot of hard work into this.

Do you have goals that you didn't meet? Failing to achieve a goal isn't entirely bad. We learn from our failures as long as we take the time to reflect on them. Think about reasons why you didn't achieve that goal. Identify what went wrong and why. You can take what you learned from this experience and use it at your next conference.

ME:

GOAL ACHIEVED (Y/N)	NEXT STEP(S)
Y	**1.** Write each of them a thank you card **2.** Stay up to date on what they are doing and provide value when I can **3.** Maintain relationship
Y	**1.** Follow-up with them **2.** Send them a copy of the book **3.** Ask them how else I can be of value to them
Y	**1.** Gather research about things that interest me **2.** Ask others what they struggle with **3.** Find areas where I can provide value **4.** Write 1,000 words per day **5.** Spend 15 minutes a day writing down ideas

GOAL ACHIEVED (Y/N) | NEXT STEP(S)

IMPLEMENT THE FOLLOW-UP

"CONTINUOUS EFFORT, NOT STRENGTH OR INTELLIGENCE, IS THE KEY TO UNLOCKING OUR POTENTIAL."
- WINSTON CHURCHILL

 Money comes and goes, but true friends always remain. Invest everything you have into your network and the relationship will be reciprocal. We could be one follow-up away from a dramatic life change, yet most of the time we don't follow-up. Why is this? The reasons are all in our head, I assure you. If you think you're too busy, you're not. You just need to prioritize better. If you think it doesn't matter, you are most likely self-sabotaging due to fear of rejection. If it feels fake, rethink your reasons for doing it and be sincere. If you think you have nothing to talk about, review the notes you took and find something. There are plenty of excuses for not taking this step, but none of them are valid.

There are tons of great ways to follow-up. You can:

1. Send an email. This may be best for the first follow-up.

2. Call them. If you exchanged numbers and you told them you'd call, pick up the phone and start dialing.

3. Send a video via email. This is a much more personal method that works really well if you're trying to build a strong relationship quickly.

4. Send a letter in the mail. This is a personal method of correspondence. If you were unable to give them a letter at the conference, sending them one in the mail is the next best thing.

5. Send them a gift. This works best with potential clients with whom you've established rapport.

Now you can complete the last four parts of the goal sheet.

YOU:

PEOPLE I MET	HOW CAN I HELP THEM	FOLLOW-UP METHOD	HOW CAN THEY HELP ME

Remember to personalize your follow-ups and show how you can help the person. When starting a business, getting a new job, or promotion, we usually remember our first supporter. Other reasons to reach out are for holidays, anniversaries, vacations, and birthdays. Be constantly aware of what your network is doing so you can always be the first to support, congratulate, or help whenever there's a chance. If you want to reach out to an influencer but are unsure how you can help, follow them on twitter or their blog. You'll be up to date on everything they're doing and it should be easy to at least come up with a way you could possibly benefit them.

The way in which you follow-up with all of the people you meet will directly correlate with how much stronger your network grows. I can't stress this enough: if you fail to follow-up after a conference, it's almost as if you were never there.

MAINTAIN YOUR NETWORK

"OUR LIFE IS FRITTERED AWAY BY DETAIL ... SIMPLIFY, SIMPLIFY."
- HENRY DAVID THOREAU

 If you do one follow-up and then lose touch, what did you really gain? Continued engagement with your network is the difference between having acquaintances and having strong relationships. Managing a network can appear overwhelming, but it's easier than you think.

Don't let yourself burn out or get stressed about keeping in touch with everyone...use what's available and make it easier on yourself. The tools below will help you do that.

RECOMMENDED TOOLS   KEY: ***= FREE

 Think and Grow Events* – is the website to find personal development conferences, webinars, and meet ups. This is growing rapidly and is an amazing place to find events that are right for you.
www.thinkandgrowevents.com

 Contactually – is a perfect tool that makes sure you never forget to follow-up with anyone, ever. The program is extremely beneficial in helping you organize your contacts into categories (buckets) and then you can apply follow-up reminder rules and tags based on their interests. This program has tons more to offer and is continuously improving. **www.contactually.com/invite/conferencecrushing**

InsideView*** – gives you insight on your competitors and partners. The tool provides you with almost everything you need to know about a company. Whenever you come across anything newsworthy that relates to a friend or their company you can reach out to them.
www.insideview.com

Newsle*** – tracks people in the news. It finds articles about you and anyone else you care about and will notify you after they are published. It also makes the process of sharing these articles with your network extremely simple.
www.newsle.com

ContentGems – is a service that makes it easier for you to share engaging content with your network. It all takes place in real time. You choose the topics and your contacts will receive the most relevant and popular information about it. It also has an integration with Bitly so you can track click-through analytics. You will always know which pieces of content people liked and didn't like so you can maximize your efforts in a particular direction.
www.contentgems.com

Boomerang on Gmail*** – is a plugin that makes sure your emails are noticed and receive responses. You have full control of when you send and receive email messages.
www.boomeranggmail.com

Rapportive*** – shares information about your contacts in your inbox.
www.rapportive.com

ANY OTHER TOOLS YOU RECOMMEND?

I'd love to hear about them. Send an email to tyler@conferencecrushing.com and share how they have helped you.

THE CONFERENCE HABIT

These 17 rules empower you to be a networking machine. Following them and taking action is now a smooth process. You've gone from walking into an event with a pocketful of business cards to walking into an event with a concrete plan and abundance mindset. From leaving events feeling unsatisfied to leaving events feeling empowered. From not knowing what to do next to taking everything to the next level.

Throughout this book we've talked about knowing the value you provide, taking action on your goals, and preparing yourself for the event with the proper mindset. Have you noticed the underlying theme for each rule? It's not about helping yourself. It's about helping other people. It's about connecting with people on a deep level. It's about providing value. When you help other people, you help yourself.

I hope the greatest lesson you take from this book is the mindset change from "What can I get" to "What can I give." The information you've learned has a wider scope than conferences or networking events.I encourage you to take the "what can I give" mindset and apply it outside of the conference arena. To change the world around you, you must change yourself first.

FOLLOW-UP WITH YOURSELF: THE CHALLENGE

Now that you've followed-up with everyone from the conference, it's time to follow-up with yourself. The only way to continuously get better and maximize all future events is to take ACTION.

MY CHALLENGE TO YOU:

1. Share this book with at least 1 friend you know it would really benefit

2. Invite them to do the challenge with you so you can both hold each other accountable

3. Create a list of 5 conferences that interest you

4. Pick 1 conference and commit

5. Read through the book to remind yourself of the 17 rules

6. Commit to using the full action guide before, during, and after the event

By taking on the challenge, you'll figure out which rules were easy for you to follow and which ones you need to work on for next time. The more conferences you attend, the better you will get. The rules will soon become second nature.

The action guide is a compilation of all the exercises and examples throughout the book. It will be of your utmost benefit to take action on the guide for all of your upcoming conferences. By following the rules and using the guide your outcome at every conference will continue to improve and you will be a true Conference Crusher.

The **"Conference Crushing Action Guide"** is available in both digital and print and is broken down into...

1. A template for filling out your Conference Crushing Bio

2. Your Conference Crushing Goal Tables

3. A template to help you get into the Conference Crushing Mindset

4. Your Don't Do's Worksheet

5. Quick reference sheet with all 17 rules

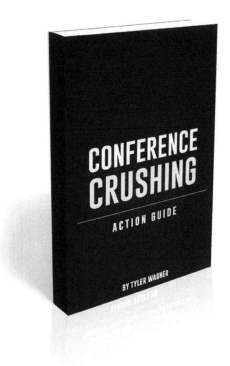

Head on over to **ConferenceCrushing.com/ActionGuide** to download the FREE Action Guide where we've done all the work for you.

ABOUT THE AUTHOR

Tyler grew up with more energy and passion than most people knew how to handle. As a kid, his vitality was contagious and he freely spread his energy and optimism. Tyler continuously found ways to push his limits as far as he could, and he refused to take the "normal path" and sit on the sidelines of his own life.

When he was a sophomore at The University of South Carolina, he started his own painting business with Young Entrepreneurs Across America. The year after that, he took on the role of mentoring five students, teaching them how to run their own successful businesses. It became apparent that helping others and showing them a different way to be "successful" was his passion. Giving others the energy and happiness to create their own path was his yellow brick road.

After this, Tyler took a leap of faith and moved to Canada to intern under Jayson Gaignard (Founder of MastermindTalks). He helped to put on multiple conferences, events, and retreats. There he learned what made an exceptional conference that delivered the most value to all of its attendees from the best of the best.

While putting on and attending tons of conferences, Tyler studied what type of attendees were getting the most out of these events. He wanted everyone to maximize their ROI at these events so he created this book, Conference Crushing.

Tyler now speaks to and consults with students, businesses, and entrepreneurs across the country, teaching them the lessons he's learned on crushing conferences, expanding networks, and nurturing relationships.

To receive a PDF with descriptions of Tyler's top speeches and more information on consulting email him at tyler@conferencecrushing.com

URGENT PLEA!

Thank you for buying the book! I really appreciate all of your feedback, and I love hearing what you have to say.

I need your input to make the next version better.

Please leave a helpful REVIEW on Amazon.com

Thanks so much!!!
-Tyler

10640460R00038

Made in the USA
San Bernardino, CA
22 April 2014